Celestial Wonders

Foundation Pieced Stellar Designs

Liz Schwartz & Stephen Seifert

Zippy Designs Publishing —— Newport, Virginia

Acknowledgments

There are stars everywhere! Throughout our lives we encounter stars in our families, communities and around the world. Stephen and I would like to especially thank our parents for being our most brilliant stars, which guide us beyond the obstacles inherent in darkness. We love you!

We also wish to thank all of our quilting friends who have encouraged us and helped us to make this project a success.

Special thanks are in order for the fabric companies who have generously donated their wonderful fabrics for the projects in this book: Hoffman International Fabrics, Robert Kaufman Fine Fabrics, and P&B Textiles. Thank you for your continuing support and belief in our work!

We dedicate this book to the quilting stars who have helped us to discover and love foundation piecing: Georgia Bonesteel, Carol Doak, Lesly Claire-Greenburg, Adrienne Johnson, and Dixie Haywood.

Liz Schwartz & Stephen Seifert
September, 1997
Newport, VA

Proudly Printed in the U.S.A. by:
Zippy Designs Publishing
Home of The Foundation Piecer
RR 1 Box 187M
Newport, VA 24128
Telephone: 540/544-7153
Fax: 540/544-7071
http://www.quiltersweb.com

Contents

Preface

Stars are a universal key to unlocking the chest of creativity swelling within everyone. Liz and I often look up into the heavens and begin to see designs hidden among the glimmering stellar tapestry, which we all can behold. In my university studies I once read something by W.B. Yeats, which has continued to inspire me:

> *Had I the heavens' embroidered cloths,*
> *Enwrought with the golden and silver light,*
> *The blue and the dim and the dark cloths*
> *Of night and light and the half-light,*
> *I would spread the cloths under your feet:*
> *But I, being poor, have only my dreams;*
> *I have spread my dreams under your feet;*
> *Tread softly because you tread on my dreams.*

Quilt blocks are fabulous to play with, since there are so many possible ways to use them. The unique designs that appear in this book also give you the option to explore the ever expanding horizon of your creativity.

While we present the *Celestial Wonders* Sampler Quilt, we hope that you will use the blocks as a starting point to develop your own quilts, which express your own visions of *Celestial Wonders*. Next time you take a stroll outside, look up into the heavens and ponder over the possibilities that are evident within the quilted sky.

Each block in this book has been stitched together in a number of options, but do not let that stop you from choosing different fabric schemes. The quilter's palette determines the feeling that a quilt conveys, which suggests that your quilt will be your expression of the glimmering worlds beyond.

Foundation Piecing Basics

Helpful Tools:

• Wooden Seam Pressing Bar

• Add-A-Quarter Ruler

Making the Foundations:

Needle Punching: Multiple foundations can be made quickly and accurately with this technique. First, trace the foundation pattern on a piece of tracing paper. Layer the traced pattern with up to 10 sheets of paper. Then, with an unthreaded sewing machine, sew along the traced lines. Repeat until you have enough foundations for the project.

Photocopying: All photocopiers will distort the image to some degree. As such, this technique is not recommended when sewing large multiple block projects. However, if photocopying is used, make sure that you always photocopy from the same original and make all of the copies needed for the project on the same machine.

Tracing: Although time consuming, tracing is an effective and accurate way to reproduce foundation patterns. A clear advantage to this technique is that it eliminates distortion.

Foundation Materials:

Muslin: When a permanent foundation is desired, the pattern can be transferred to a fabric foundation. When the project is finished this foundation will not be removed. However, it should be noted that the extra layer may make hand quilting the finished project more difficult.

Paper: Just about any type of paper will make a suitable foundation material. However, we have found that using a special semi-

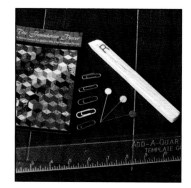

Clockwise: Postcard, Wooden Seam Pressing Bar, Vinyl Coated Paper Clips, Pins, Add-A-Quarter Ruler.

To test the accuracy of a photocopier, make a copy of the pattern. Then place the copy over the original and hold them up to a light source. You will be able to see how closely the copy matches the original.

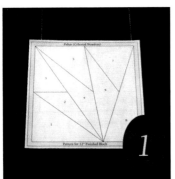

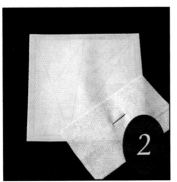

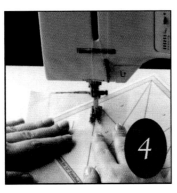

transparent paper, called Easy Piece™ Foundation Paper, works quite well. This paper is translucent allowing you to see through the paper easily and simply tears out when no longer needed.

Cutting:

The fabric patches can be prepared using two basic techniques:

Freezer Paper Templates: Trace the pattern shape, adding at least a 1/4" seam allowance all around the patch, onto freezer paper. Iron the templates onto your fabric and use them as rough cutting guides to cut pattern pieces. Peel off the template and reuse! The advantage of this technique is that is allows you to cut the pieces on the grain of the fabric, which is especially helpful when working with directional fabrics, plaids and stripes.

Fabric Strips: Instead of cutting out the specific shape of the piece, various strips of fabric are cut and used in piecing the blocks. To determine the width of the strip to cut, measure the width of the widest section of the piece and add 3/4" to that measurement. While this method uses more fabric, it is much faster and easier then using freezer paper templates.

Sewing:

Prepare your sewing machine by reducing the stitch length to 18-20 stitches per inch and changing your needle to a size 90/14. Replace the needle before you start a new project. Also, be sure not to use steam in your iron as this may cause the foundation to shrink or distort.

1.) Prepare all of the foundations that you will need for your project; using either the template or strip method cut the fabric patches. Before you cut the fabric for the entire project, it is a good idea to make a test block first.

2.) Place your first fabric piece right side up on the wrong side (unprinted) of your first paper foundation. Check to see if the fabric will cover the area by holding up the paper and the fabric to a light source (printed side of foundation facing you). Make sure that the fabric covers the entire area! Pin or glue (using a dab of glue from a glue-stick) in place.

3.) Next, place the second piece of fabric right side down on top of the first. Position the fabric so that it extends approximately 1/4" past the sewing line and pin in place. Hold the foundation and fabric up to a light source so that you can see the sewing line and check to see that the piece is positioned correctly. Pinch the fabric in place and flip it over so you can see if it covers the entire area, including seam allowances.

4.) Flip the foundation over (with the fabrics in place) to the printed side and sew on the line between the first and second pieces. Extend your line of stitching at least 1/4" before and after the printed line.

5.) Fold the fabric over into place and press gently with an iron. Or, you can use a wooden pressing bar to crease the seams and help to make it lie flat.

6.) Align a postcard, or straight edge, along the next sewing line. Crease the paper and fold it over the card revealing the fabric below.

7.) Place the Add A Quarter ruler on the crease so that it is aligned with the 1/2" lip, then trim away the excess fabric leaving a 1/4" seam allowance. Alternatively, you can use an acrylic ruler for this step; just be sure to trim 1/4" away from the crease.

8.) Align the next piece along the pre-trimmed edge. Continue adding patches in numerical order until the foundation is covered.

9.) Using a small stitch, baste around the entire foundation within the 1/4" seam allowance.

10.) After the block is completed, trim away the excess fabric and paper from the foundation. Do not remove the paper from the blocks until after they have been assembled.

The Celestial Wonders Blocks:

The beauty of these stellar designs lies in their versatility. There are a myriad of different patterns that can be made by varying the color placement and rotation of the block subunits. As such, we have intentionally excluded color guides on the foundations. Before you piece your block, make a few copies of the foundation and color them in with markers or pencils. Try a few combinations until you come to one that strikes you. Then, mark your final choices on the foundations.

Each of the *Celestial Wonders* blocks is made up of four squares. In order to make each block, you will need to make four of each of the foundation units for the block. Then, the subunits are assembled to make the finished block.

Assembling the Blocks:

11.) Lay out the four quarters of the block and arrange them to make the finished design. Try experimenting with the way that the units are placed for more block possibilities!

12.) Identify several key match points and place pins through them (like corners and center seams) so that the pin passes perpendicularly through the sewing lines (the inner line on the paper foundation) of both blocks. When the block subunits are aligned, fasten them together using several vinyl coated paper clips. After the paper clips are set, remove all of the pins.

13.) Sew the units together being careful to remove the paper clips as you sew.

14.) Press the seams open on the block halves to reduce the bulkiness where many seams join.

15.) Sew the two block halves together to make the completed block. Leave the paper on the back of the block until the sashing has been attached and you are ready to quilt your project.

Finishing:

When the quilt top is completed and you are ready to quilt it, remove the paper foundations from the back of all of the blocks. If you have trouble removing it, try using a pair of tweezers to get into the tight spots. Moistening the paper, or gently scraping it with your fingernail also helps to coax difficult pieces to come off. You might also try soaking the whole piece in water; when the paper gets wet it will fall right off. However, be careful not to clog your sink or washing machine with paper. If you have used muslin foundations, they will not be removed and will become a permanent part of the quilt.

Quilting:

To prepare your top for quilting, layer it with the batting and backing, then baste the layers together by hand. Hand or machine quilt as desired. Some possibilities might be to stitch in the ditch, outlining each star shape, stippling the entire quilt or creating a unique star quilting pattern to accent your blocks. Using metallic or specialty threads would add some extra dimension to your finished piece. See the *Suggested Reading* list for some wonderful quilting titles to learn more about methods to quilt your project.

Binding:

Either purchase or make enough french fold bias binding to finish the edges of your quilt. Attach the binding to the quilt A straight binding may also be used if desired. For more information on how to finish up the quilt, see the Suggested Reading list to find a title with more detailed explanations of binding and finishing your quilting project.

Suggested Reading

Binding/Finishing:

Happy Endings: Finishing the Edges of Your Quilt by Mimi Dietrich
That Patchwork Place

Taking the Math Out of Making Patchwork Quilts by Bonnie Leman and Judy Martin
Leman Publications, Inc.

General Reference:

Quilter's Complete Guide by Marianne Fons & Liz Porter
Oxmoor House

Quilting:

Machine Quilting Made Easy by Maurine Noble
That Patchwork Place

Quilting by Machine
Singer Sewing Reference Library
Cy DeCosse, Inc.

Quilting Makes the Quilt by Lee Cleland
That Patchwork Place

Quilting with Style: Principals for Great Pattern Design by Gwen Marston and Joe Cunningham
American Quilter's Society

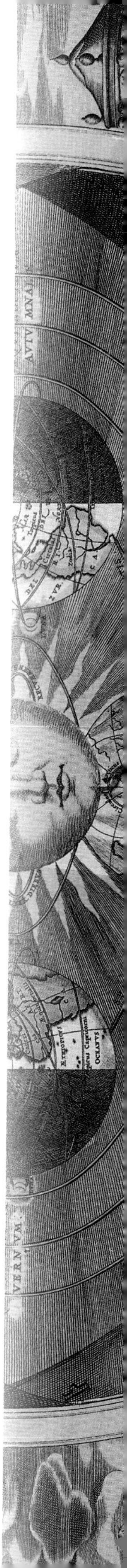

Desired Finished Block Size
4".........Reduce 33%
6".........Reduce 50%
8".........Reduce 66%
14".....Enlarge 116%
16".....Enlarge 133%
18".....Enlarge 150%

Changing the Finished Block Size:

The foundations for the *Celestial Wonders* blocks are provided in a 12" finished size. However, they may be easily resized for use in many other projects. The most convenient way is to use the reducing and enlarging functions that can be found on most copiers. Since copiers may distort the image when the size change is made, it is advisable to check the resized foundation to see that it is the right size before you start sewing your project.

In order to obtain the common block sizes shown on the left, set your copy machine to the indicated settings and then copy the foundation image provided for the block that is desired.

Sources:

Most of the tools and materials used to make the projects in this book may be found at your favorite quilt shop. However, if you find that you cannot locate them, they are available from:

Zippy Designs Publishing

Home of *The Foundation Piecer*

RR 1 Box 187M

Newport, VA 24128

Items Available:

- Add-A-Quarter Ruler
- Easy Piece™ Foundation Paper
- Wooden Seam Pressing Bar

Celestial Wonders

Block Patterns

Apogee

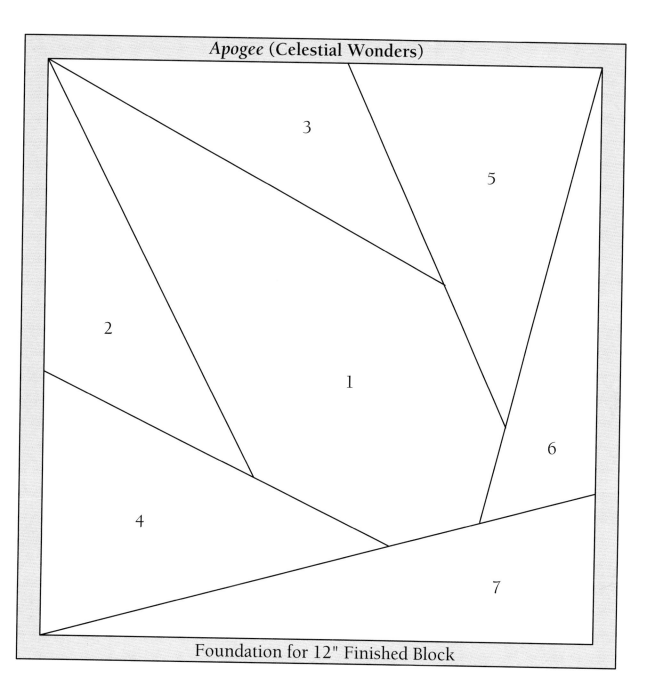

Apogee (Celestial Wonders)

3

5

2

1

6

4

7

Foundation for 12" Finished Block

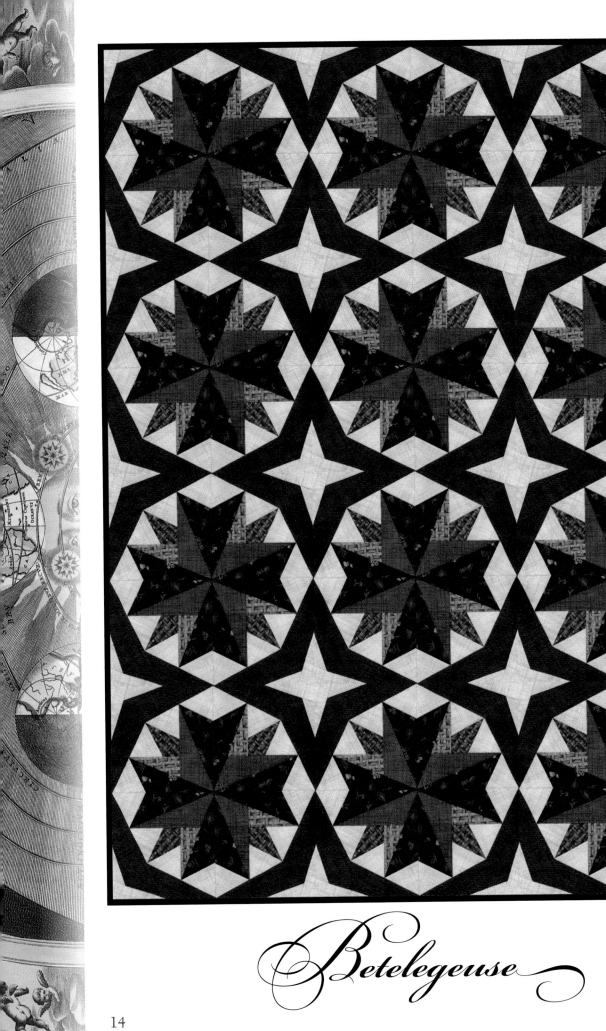

Betelegeuse

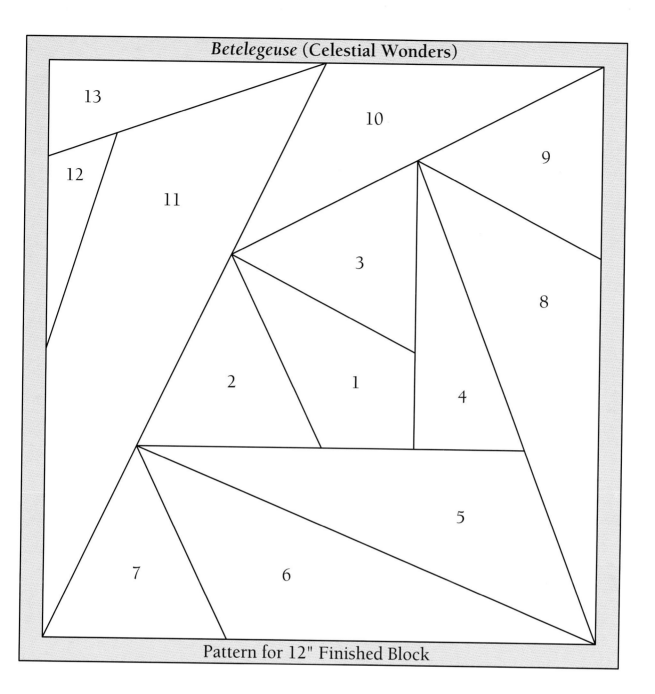

Betelegeuse (Celestial Wonders)

13

12

11

10

9

3

8

2   1

4

5

7   6

Pattern for 12" Finished Block

Black Hole

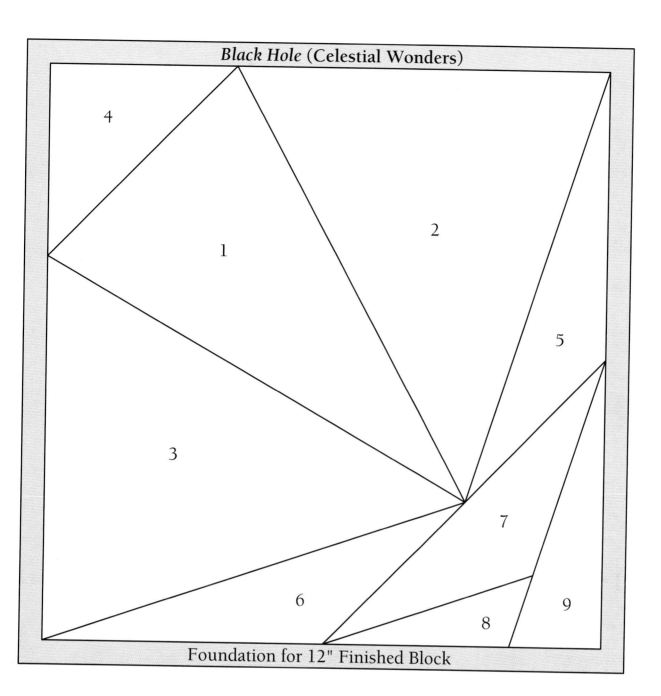

Black Hole (Celestial Wonders)

4

1

2

5

3

7

6

8

9

Foundation for 12" Finished Block

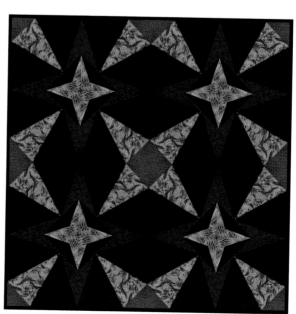

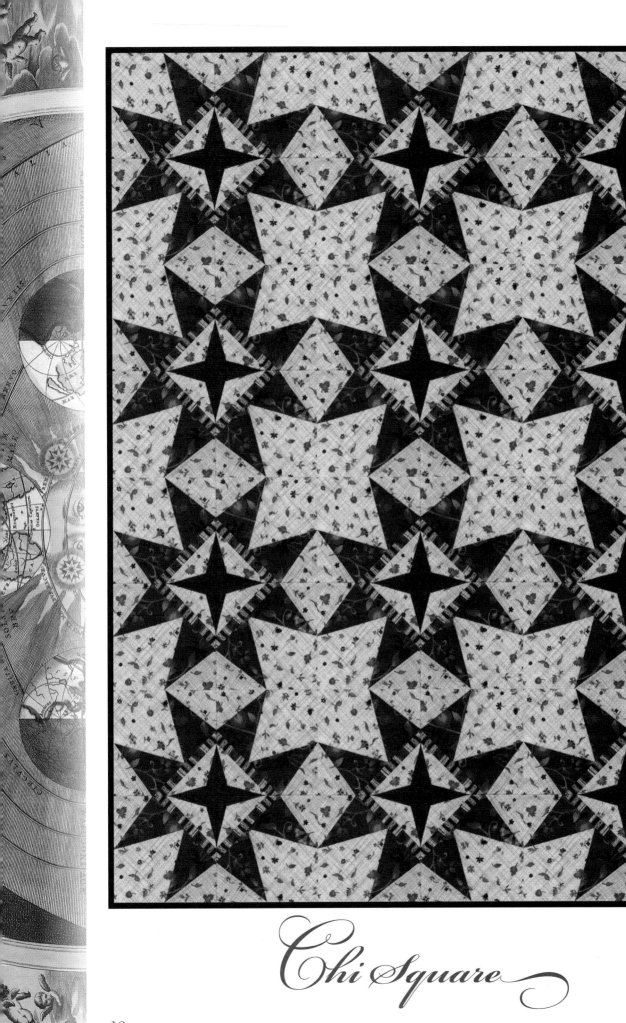

Chi Square

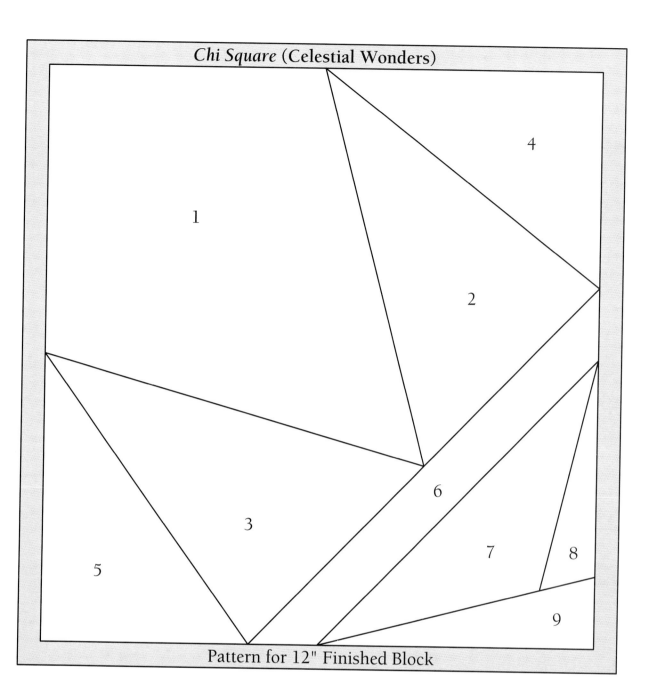

Chi Square (Celestial Wonders)

1

4

2

6

3

5

7

8

9

Pattern for 12" Finished Block

Galaxy

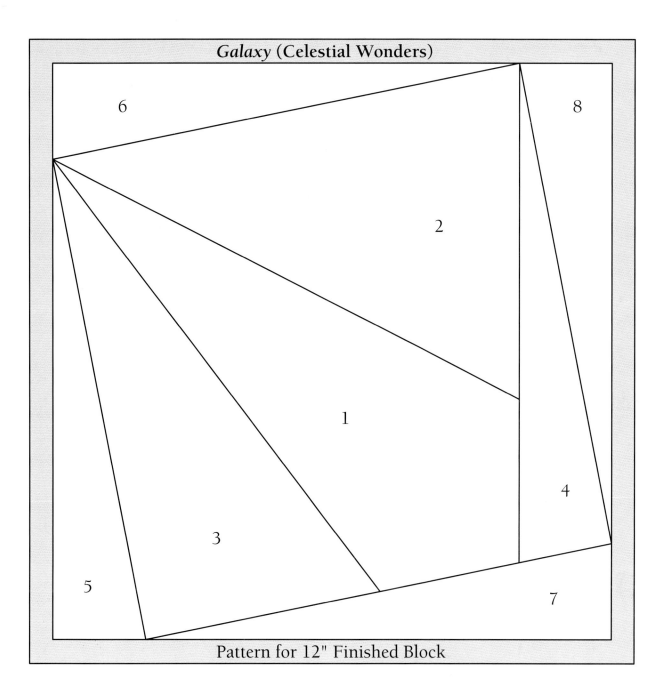

Galaxy (Celestial Wonders)

6

8

2

1

4

3

5

7

Pattern for 12" Finished Block

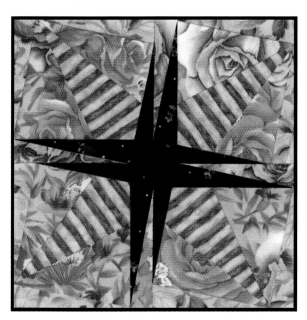

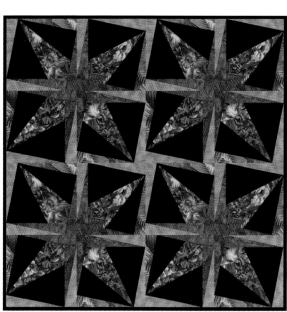

Midnight Sun

22

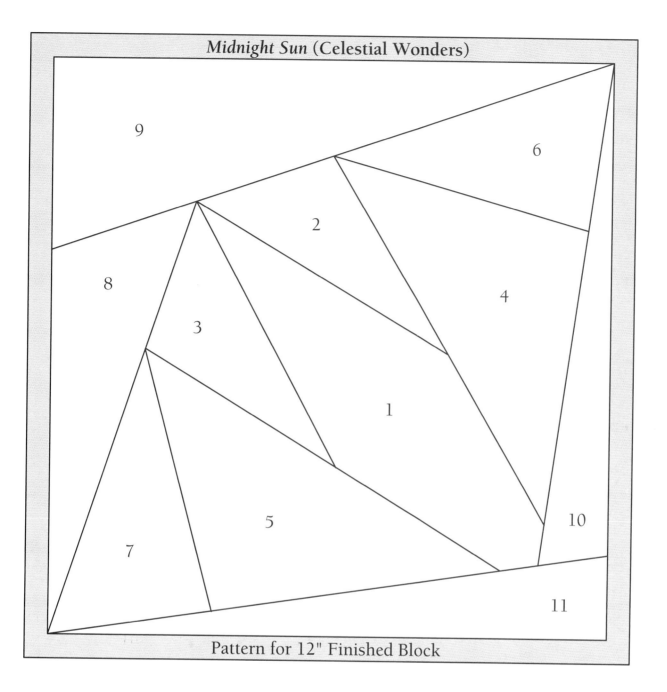

Midnight Sun (Celestial Wonders)

9

6

2

8

4

3

1

5

10

7

11

Pattern for 12" Finished Block

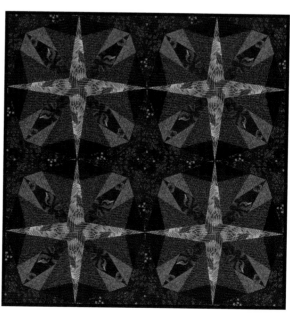

Peony

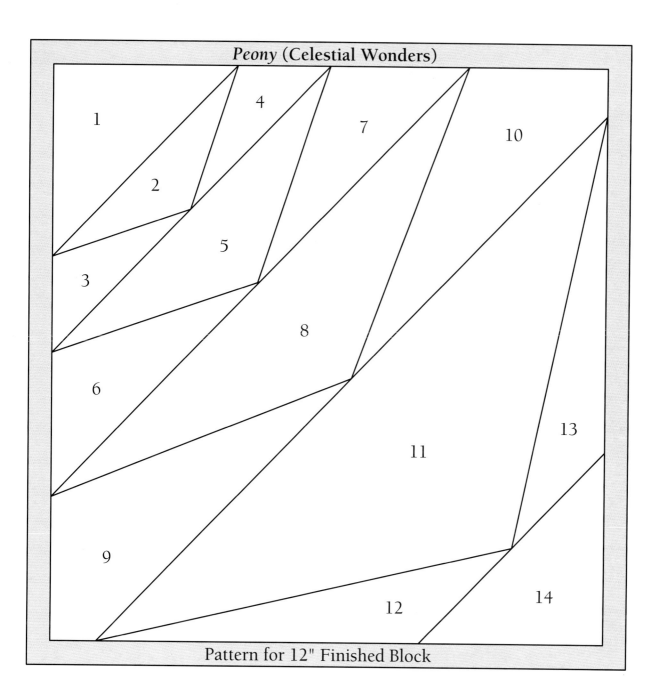

Peony (Celestial Wonders)

1

4

2

7

10

5

3

8

6

13

11

9

14

12

Pattern for 12" Finished Block

Polaris

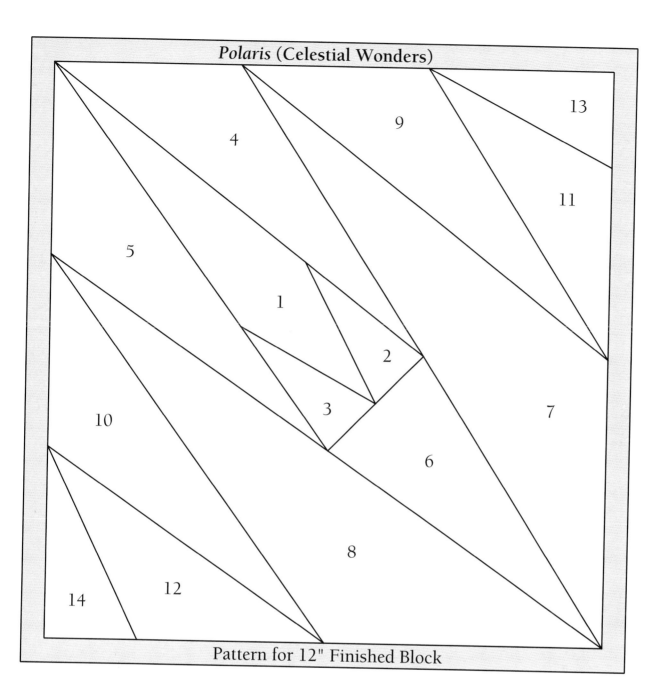

Polaris (Celestial Wonders)

4

13

9

11

5

1

2

3

7

10

6

8

14

12

Pattern for 12" Finished Block

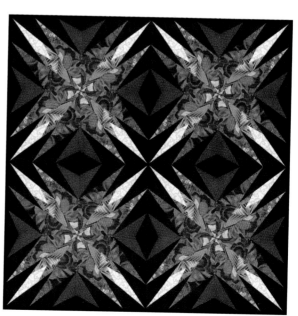

Pulsar

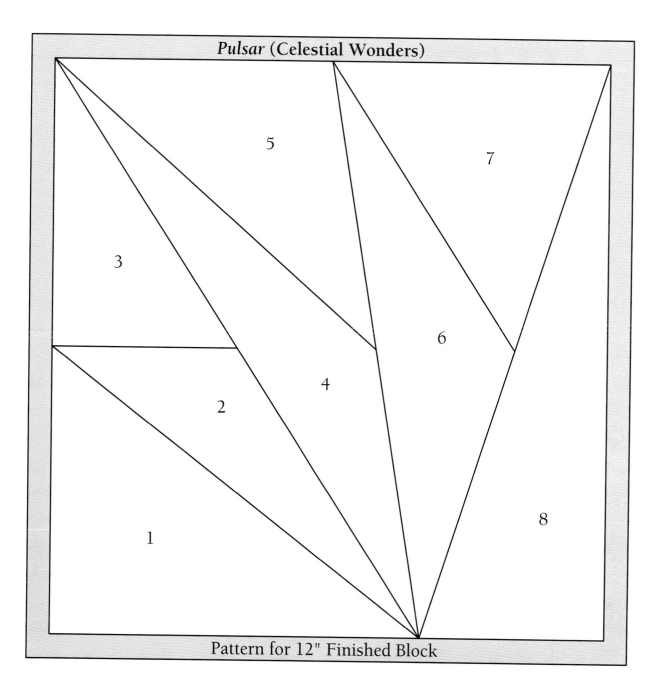

Pulsar (Celestial Wonders)

5

3

7

6

4

2

1

8

Pattern for 12" Finished Block

Quasar

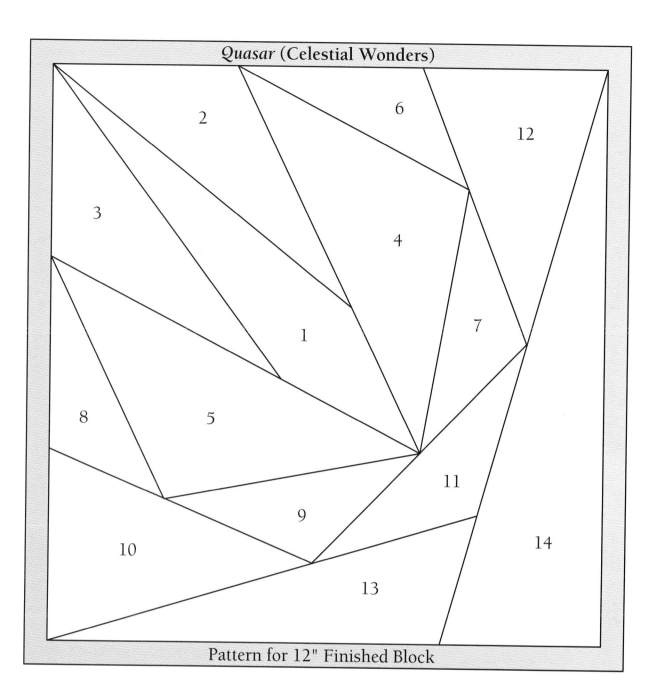

Quasar (Celestial Wonders)

2

6

12

3

4

1

7

8

5

11

9

14

10

13

Pattern for 12" Finished Block

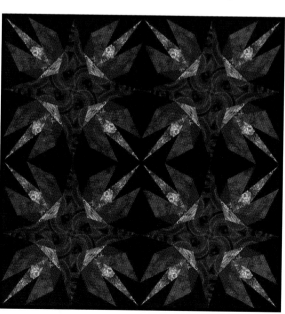

Supernova

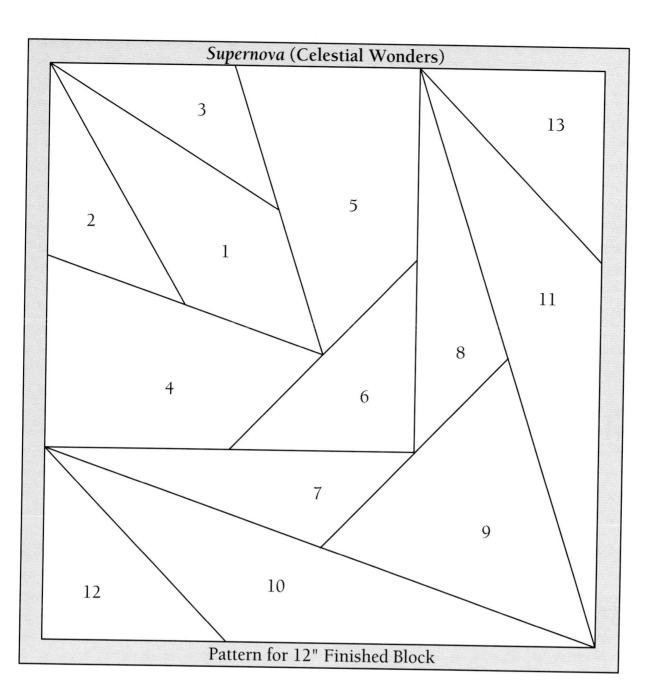

Supernova (Celestial Wonders)

3

13

2

5

1

11

8

4

6

7

9

12

10

Pattern for 12" Finished Block

White Dwarf

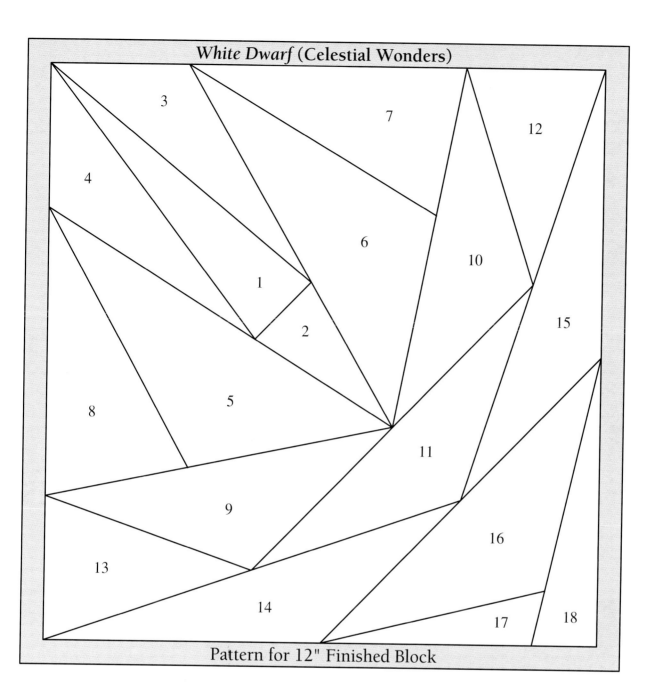

White Dwarf (Celestial Wonders)

3

7

12

4

1

6

2

10

15

8

5

11

9

16

13

14

17

18

Pattern for 12" Finished Block

Celestial Wonders

Sampler Quilt

Fabrics from the Folklore Collecion by P&B Textiles

Sampler Quilt Project

Star designs have always been popular with quilters since the birth of quilting itself. This sampler features a dozen original interpretations of the ever loved star that challenges you to see this time honored designs in new ways.

Each block can be used alone to make a quilt, as well as making a sampler. While the blocks shown in the sampler quilts in this book are arranged alphabetically, feel free to experiment and arrange them any way you choose! If you choose to explore new layout options you may consider a medallion style quilt and vary the sizes of the finished blocks. The most essential thing for you to remember is that you are the real star when making your *Celestial Wonders* Sampler quilt!

Approximate Finished Size: 48" X 63"

With additional borders to enlarge quilt:

- Twin: 66" X 81"
- Full/Queen: 84" X 99"

Yardage Requirements:

For 48" X 63" Quilt:

2 1/2 yds. Feature Fabric (Cornerstones, Sashing, and Blocks)

2 yds. Background (Blocks)

1/4 yd. each of 12-18 fabrics that coordinate with the Feature Fabric for piecing the *Celestial Wonders* blocks. Choose an assortment of lights, mediums and darks.

Additional Materials for the Twin Quilt:

1 3/4 yds. Border Fabric

Additional Materials for the Full/Queen Quilt:

4 1/2 yds. Border Fabric

Cutting:

🖋 Cut (31) 3 1/2" X 12 1/2" strips from the Feature Fabric for the sashing. Set aside.

For the Twin Quilt:

🖋 Cut (7) 9 1/2" X 44" strips from the border fabric. Set aside.

For the Full/Queen Quilt:

🖋 Cut (7) 18 1/2" X 44" strips from the border fabric. Set aside.

If using solid Cornerstones:

🖋 Cut (20) 3 1/2" X 3 1/2" squares. Set aside.

Assembly:

▷ Sew (1) each of all of the *Celestial Wonders* blocks. Use the *Coloring Diagram* showing the completed quilt to plan your color and fabric choices.

▷ Make (20) Cornerstone blocks. Note that each cornerstone requires (4) foundation units to make one block. You will need a total of (80) foundation units to make (20) completed blocks.

▷ Arrange the blocks, cornerstones and sashing to make the quilt design. Then sew everything together as shown in the Coloring Diagram to make the completed quilt top. The heavy red lines in the diagram show the major sections.

Borders:

No additional borders are needed for a Crib Quilt/Lab Quilt. If you are making either the Twin or Full/Queen Quilt then you will need to add the outer borders:

▷ Measure the length of the finished top.

▷ Piece the border strips together and cut (2) pieces the same size as the measurement of the length of the quilt top. Sew the strips to the long sides of the top.

▷ Measure the width of the top and bottom of the quilt after the side border strips have been added.

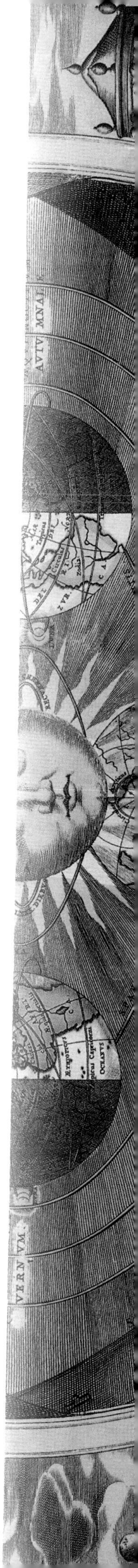

☞ Piece the border strips together and cut (2) pieces the same size as the measurement of the width of the quilt top. Sew the strips to the top and bottom of the quilt top.

Finishing:

☞ Remove the paper from the back of all of the blocks.

☞ Layer the quilt top with backing and batting. Using a 100% cotton batting will give your finished quilt a soft, antique feel.

☞ Hand or machine quilt as desired.

☞ Bind using your favorite method.

Celestial Wonders Sampler Quilt
Cornerstone Foundations

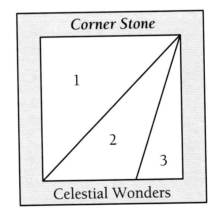

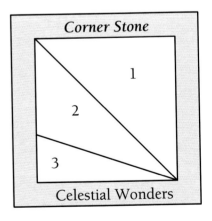

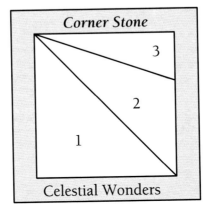

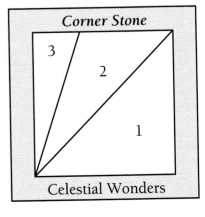

Celestial Wonders Sampler Quilt Coloring Diagram

Celestial Wonders

Quilt Gallery

Starry, Starry Quilt

Monet's Celestial Garden

Fabrics from the Sweet Rose Collection by Robert Kaufman Fine Fabrics

Kyoto Skies

Blocks Used: Apogee and Galaxy

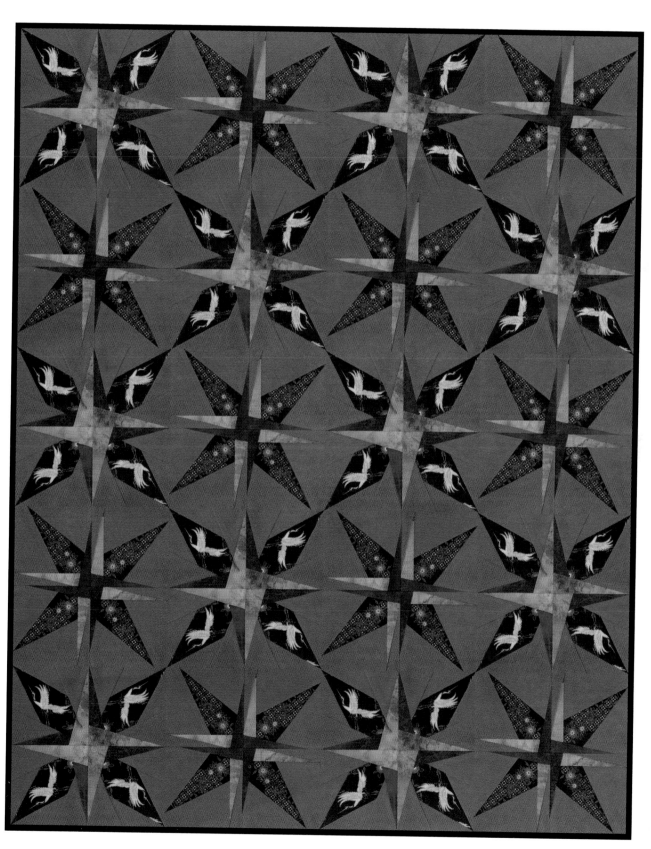

Let it Snow

Blocks Used: Betelgeuse and Supernova

Heaven above the Tropics

Block Used: Peony

Epilogue

We hope that you have enjoyed stitching up these stellar designs! Half of these patterns originally appeared in *The Foundation Piecer, The Pattern Journal for Quilters Who Love Foundation Piecing*. Published bimonthly, each full color issue features 12-15 projects ranging from time honored tradtional patterns to contemporary art quilts.

We invite you to share in the fun and would love to see pictures of your stellar quilts. Until next time, happy sewing!

Liz & Stephen

Subscribe to The Foundation Piecer Today!

☐ **Sample Issue**
Only $6.00

☐ **One-Year Subscription (6 Issues)**
Only $ 30.00

Name: _____

Address: _____

City, State, Zip: _____

Phone/e-mail: _____

Visa/MC: _____ Exp. _____

Zippy Designs Publishing
The Foundation Piecer
RFD#1 Box 187M
Newport, VA 24128
Orders: 888/544-7153
Fax: 540/544-7071

International subscribers: A one year subscription is $36.00 surface, $60.00 Air and sample issues are $7.00 surface, $12.00 Air. U.S. Funds Only. Please don't cut me up! You can send your name, address and payment without this form to the address above if you wish. Telephone: (540)544-7153. Web Site *http://www.quiltersweb.com*